YOUR KNOWLEDGE HAS VALUE

- We will publish your bachelor's and master's thesis, essays and papers

- Your own eBook and book - sold worldwide in all relevant shops

- Earn money with each sale

Upload your text at www.GRIN.com
and publish for free

Bibliographic information published by the German National Library:

The German National Library lists this publication in the National Bibliography; detailed bibliographic data are available on the Internet at http://dnb.dnb.de .

This book is copyright material and must not be copied, reproduced, transferred, distributed, leased, licensed or publicly performed or used in any way except as specifically permitted in writing by the publishers, as allowed under the terms and conditions under which it was purchased or as strictly permitted by applicable copyright law. Any unauthorized distribution or use of this text may be a direct infringement of the author s and publisher s rights and those responsible may be liable in law accordingly.

Imprint:

Copyright © 2016 GRIN Verlag, Open Publishing GmbH
Print and binding: Books on Demand GmbH, Norderstedt Germany
ISBN: 9783668263840

This book at GRIN:

http://www.grin.com/en/e-book/336016/lady-macbeth-king-duncan-and-the-witches-why-are-the-characters-of-shakespeare-s

Rebekka Lohse

Lady Macbeth, King Duncan and the Witches. Why are the characters of Shakespeare's "Macbeth" still discussed today?

GRIN Publishing

GRIN - Your knowledge has value

Since its foundation in 1998, GRIN has specialized in publishing academic texts by students, college teachers and other academics as e-book and printed book. The website www.grin.com is an ideal platform for presenting term papers, final papers, scientific essays, dissertations and specialist books.

Visit us on the internet:

http://www.grin.com/

http://www.facebook.com/grincom

http://www.twitter.com/grin_com

List of Contents

1 Introduction 2
2 Biography of William Shakespeare 2
3 Summary of *Macbeth* 4
4 Covered Characters 6
    4.1 Macbeth 6
    4.2 Lady Macbeth 7
    4.3 King Duncan 8
    4.4 Three Witches or Weïrd Sisters 8
5 Conclusion 9
Sources 11

1 Introduction

If you type "William Shakespeare" into Google you will receive over 64 million results. And, although very little is known about his personal life the plays and poems he wrote have survived over four centuries and Shakespeare's works are the second most quoted after the Bible. This research paper will be focusing on "one of Shakespeare's most enduringly popular and globally influential plays"[1]: the tragedy *Macbeth*. The play was probably written around 1606. The play focuses on a Thane called Macbeth who is driven by witches and by his wife into the murder of King Duncan in order to take the throne for himself. Since 1606 *Macbeth* has been performed uncountable times in theatres and screened several times, the most recent one being *Macbeth* (UK, 2015) with Justin Kurzel directing and Michael Fassbender starring as Macbeth. Shakespeare's plays, such as *Macbeth,* are still addressed in schools around the world. The following study focuses on the characters of Macbeth, Lady Macbeth, King Duncan and the Witches or Weïrd Sisters. The main focus being why they are still discussed today. What makes the conflicted characters of Macbeth and Lady Macbeth so interesting? What do the witches represent? Is King Duncan a weak or generous King? At the time *Macbeth* was enjoyed by rich and poor and still is appreciated today, but why?

For this research paper the works of Bünsch, Moschovakis and Mühlmann were used.

Characters like Macduff, Malcolm and Banquo will be excluded. Also excluded will be the thesis that *Macbeth* has no beginning, middle or end because that does not relate to the research question.

2 Biography of William Shakespeare

Most historians presume that William Shakespeare was born near or on the 23rd April 1564, as there are church records of his baptism on the 26th April of the same year in Stratford-upon-Avon, England. His parents were John and Mary Shakespeare. William Shakespeare was one of six children. Before Shakespeare's birth, his father had become a successful merchant and a public official. Very little is known about William Shakespeare, the man who is credited for 38 plays, 154 sonnets, and two

---

[1] Moschovakis, Nick: Introduction. Dualistic *Macbeth*? Problematic *Macbeth*?. in: Moschovakis, Nick (Hrsg.): Macbeth. New critical essays, Routledge, New York 2008, S. 1

narrative poems, which often raises questions about the authorship of his plays. There even is some debate about whether or not Shakespeare even existed.

There are only minimal records regarding Shakespeare's childhood and education. Historians suppose that he most likely attended the King's New School in Stanford. On the 28th November 1582, William Shakespeare married Anne Hathaway, with whom he had three children: two daughters and a son, who died at the age of 11.

Historians refer to the seven years that followed as 'the lost years' as there are no records of what was happening to the Shakespeare family. On the 20th September 1592 edition of the *Stationers' Register* Robert Greene, a London playwright, wrote the following of Shakespeare "...There is an upstart Crow, beautified with our feathers, that with his Tiger's heart wrapped in a Player's hide, supposes he is as well able to bombast out a blank verse as the best of you: and being an absolute Johannes factotum, is in his own conceit the only Shake-scene in a country,"[2] This proves that Shakespeare was known as an actor and playwright in London by 1592. There are also documents that show that Shakespeare was a managing partner in a London acting company called the Lord Chamberlain's Men. The company most likely performed Shakespeare's *Henry VI* series, *Richard III* and *The Comedy of Errors* between 1590 and 1592. It is thought that Shakespeare possibly started writing most of his sonnets around 1593, of which 154 still well respected to this day.

Shakespeare's plays were very popular with the London Masses and Lords. The Lord Chamberlain's Men often performed before the court of Queen Elizabeth I. Because of his success, Shakespeare was able to purchase the second largest house in Stratford in 1597 for his wife and children. In 1599, Shakespeare and others from the Lord Chamberlain's Men established the Globe Theatre. The company changed their name to the King's Men when King James I was crowned in 1603. It is believed that during King James I's reign, Shakespeare wrote many of his most accomplished plays about courtly power, including *King Lear*, *Macbeth*, and *Antony and Cleopatra*.

William Shakespeare died on the 23rd April 1616 in Stratford-upon-Avon, leaving most of his estate to his oldest daughter.

---

[2] http://www.biography.com/people/william-shakespeare-9480323, letzter Zugriff: 06.01, 17:30

3 Summary of *Macbeth*

Act 1

The play begins with three witches who plan to meet Macbeth after a battle. In the next scene, the audience is introduced to the royal household: King Duncan, Malcolm and Donaldbain. At the beginning of *Macbeth,* the King of Norway is invading Scotland. A captain who has been wounded in battle reports to King Duncan that Macbeth and Banquo fought bravely against the Norwegian troops and the troops of the traitor Macdonald, who Macbeth personally killed. King Duncan praises both Macbeth and Banquo. Ross reports to King Duncan that Macbeth has triumphed and that another traitor, the Thane of Cawdor, has been captured. King Duncan sentences the Thane of Cawdor to death and awards his titles to Macbeth, which is to be celebrated at Macbeth's castle. After the battle, the three witches plot evil deeds while awaiting Macbeth. When Banquo and Macbeth arrive the witches foretell that Macbeth will be Thane of Cawdor and King of Scotland. The witches also prophesy that Banquo will not be king but his descendants will. After the witches disappear Ross arrives reporting that King Duncan was delighted to hear about their victory and that Macbeth is now Thane of Cawdor. After the execution of Cawdor, King Duncan greets Macbeth and praises him and Banquo and declares that his son, Malcolm, will succeed to the throne. At Macbeth's castle, Lady Macbeth reads a letter from her husband, telling of the recent events. Lady Macbeth fears that Macbeth is too decent to kill King Duncan. At the arrival of Macbeth, Lady Macbeth urges him to kill King Duncan and after several quarrels, they devise a plan to kill the king.

Act 2

Macbeth kills King Duncan while hallucinating. Macbeth feels guilty but Lady Macbeth plans an alibi. After having a conversation with the porter, Macduff discovers the dead King Duncan. Macbeth, Lady Macbeth, Macduff and Banquo are all horrified. After they hear the terrible news Malcolm and Donaldbain, suspecting danger, decide to flee: Malcolm to England and Donaldbain to Ireland. While Ross is discussing strange events that mirror Duncan's murder, Macduff tells him that Duncan's sons have fled and, therefore, Macbeth has been elected King of Scotland.

Act 3

Banquo starts fearing that Macbeth has become king by evil means. Macbeth requests that Banquo and his son, Fleance, are present at the banquet. Macbeth plans to have both killed as he fears his claim to the throne, although Lady Macbeth urges him not to. The murderers kill Banquo but Fleance manages to escape. The news that Banquo had been killed but his sons managed to escape, do not satisfy Macbeth. As Macbeth welcomes his guests he starts to see Banquo's ghost, causing create confusion between the lords. Macbeth vows to revisit the witches and to kill anyone who stands between him and the throne.

Act 4

Macbeth visits the Witches and demands to know the future. The three Witches show him three Apparitions: An armed head, a bloody child and a child crowned with a tree in his hand. The Apparitions tell him to be aware of Macduff, that no man born of women can harm him and that he will only be defeated when Birnam Wood comes to Dunsinane. Lennox informs Macbeth that Macduff has fled to England thus Macbeth decides to kill Macduff's family. Lady Macduff tries to explain the absence of their father to her children shortly before all are murdered. In England, Malcolm tests Macduff to be sure of his loyalty. Malcolm declares he will invade Scotland. Ross informs Malcolm and Macduff that in Scotland a rebellion against Macbeth is rumoured, he also tells Macduff of the slaughter of his family. Macduff vows to avenge his wife and children.

Act 5

Lady Macbeth suffers greatly because of her guilt. While sleepwalking she speaks of the murders that Macbeth has committed. Malcolm and Macduff with the English army are approaching Macbeth and many Scottish young men are joining them. Macbeth vows to fight until he dies. Malcolm orders his army to use the branches of Birnam Wood as camouflage in order to approach Dunsinane. Macbeth is informed of Lady Macbeth's death and that Birnam Wood is coming to Dunsinane. While fighting Macduff Macbeth boasts that no man born of women can kill but Macduff reveals that as cut from his mother's womb. Macduff kills Macbeth and hails Malcolm as the new King of Scotland.

4 Covered Characters

In the following I will analyse the characters that I find to be most relevant and the themes discussed.

4.1 Macbeth

Macbeth is the main character and the title figure of *Macbeth*. At the beginning of the play, he is a war hero, whose loyalty is questioned when three witches prophesy that he will become king. His ambitious wife, Lady Macbeth, then persuades him to murder King Duncan even though Macbeth is still torn between loyalty and treason. After the murder of King Duncan, Macbeth kills several others, like his friend Banquo and Macduff's family. He shifts between cruel confidence "O, full of scorpions is my mind," (Act 3, Scene 2, Line 36 [3.2.36]) and guilt "Who should against his murderer shut the door, / Not bear the knife myself (1.7.15-16) At the end of the play, Macduff decapitates him. Macbeth is the hero and the villain of the play.[3]

In *Macbeth,* there are several paradoxes "So foul and fair a day I have not seen" (1.3.36) and nothing is what it seems "look like th'inncocent flower, / But be the serpent under't" (1.6.63-64). According to Nick Moschovakis, this imagery is used to "throw doubt on our ability to distinguish 'good' from 'evil'."[4] Or the play could, on the other hand, teach us the lesson that we must distinguish between the two. *Macbeth* also explores the theme that the temptations of evil that defeat even the strongest people. This idea and the theme that evil is often not easy to recognise still intrigues audiences to this day.

Even though Macbeth would not have murdered King Duncan without the influence of his wife and the witches, he still is a very ambitious man and is willing to do anything to sustain his power. Perhaps Shakespeare wishes to imply that the lust for power ultimately brings great unhappiness and ruin.[5] Throughout the play, Macbeth struggles between ambition and self-doubt. Shakespeare might have used Macbeth to show how ambition and guilt can destroy people who lack the necessary character strength. This topic is still discussed today.

---

[3] http://www.cummingsstudyguides.net/xMacbeth.html, letzter Zugriff: 03.01.2016, 16:30
[4] Moschovakis, Nick: Introduction. Dualistic *Macbeth*? Problematic *Macbeth*?. in: Moschovakis, Nick (Hrsg.): Macbeth. New critical essays, Routledge, New York 2008, S. 2
[5] http://www.cummingsstudyguides.net/xMacbeth.html, letzter Zugriff: 03.01.2016, 16:30

4.2 Lady Macbeth

At the beginning of the play Lady Macbeth seems, even more, ambitious and cruel than her husband "That I may pour my spirits in thine ear; / And chastise with the valour of my tongue / All that impedes thee from the golden round," (1.5.24-26) Later the audience learns that Lady Macbeth actually needs alcohol in order to be this straight forward. "That which hath made them drunk hath made me bold; / What hath quench'd them hath given me fire." (2.2.1-2) Because of her guilt, Lady Macbeth commits suicide.

In Shakespeare's lifetime women were mainly seen as the weaker sex and it was also thought that it was the will of God that they obeyed and served either their father, brother or, when married, their husband. The biggest event in a woman's life was her marriage. After the marriage, women were supposed to take care of the household and give birth to many children. The most famous woman of this age was Queen Elizabeth I. [6]

Because Lady Macbeth is such a complex character, she is ultimately one of Shakespeare's most famous female characters. [7] The theme of guilt is not only explored in the character of Macbeth but also in the character of Lady Macbeth. "Out, damned spot" (5.1.30) Lady Macbeth is undone by her guilt. She sleepwalks around the castle, nagged by hallucinations just before she takes her own life. The character of Lady Macbeth seems to teach the lesson that evil deeds don't lead to a happy future. Lady Macbeth could on the other hand, also be a praise to powerful women like Queen Elizabeth I. [8] What her husband lacks in strength, ambition and ruthlessness, Lady Macbeth embraces with pride even though, as mentioned before, women at the time were meant to be weak and obedient and not ambitious as well as violent. When Macbeth doesn't want to go through with the murder she overrides his disapproval by questioning his manhood. This shows that Lady Macbeth uses other people in order to achieve her ambitious goals, which she can't achieve on her own, a trade that still fascinates audiences to this day. However, she is not cold-blooded enough to keep hold of her achievements, which inevitably leads to her losing her

---

[6] http://www.william-shakespeare.info/elizabethan-women.htm, letzter Zugriff: 10.01.2016, 11:15
[7] http://www.sparknotes.com/shakespeare/macbeth/canalysis.html, letzter Zugriff: 04.01.2016, 18:10
[8] http://www.sparknotes.com/shakespeare/macbeth/canalysis.html, letzter Zugriff: 04.01.2016, 18:10

sanity. Lady Macbeth changes from a manipulative to a subtle and later to a crazed woman.

4.3 King Duncan

King Duncan only appears in Act 1 and is presented, according to Rebecca Lemon, as a "grateful leader and a father figure."[9] King Duncan awards the title of Thane of Cawdor to Macbeth and travels to Macbeth's castle in order to celebrate this. King Duncan is murdered off-stage in Act 2.

Nature plays a big part in *Macbeth*. Natural imagery of fertility (1.4.32-33) underlines Duncan's divine right to rule. Macbeth however, is surrounded by dark and foul imagery (1.5.38, 2.1.50). This contrast shows how different the two are, King Duncan rules through love and Macbeth through fear. Whilst Macbeth is king Macduff states "each new morn / New widows howl, new orphans cry" (4.3.4-5), showing that the fear soon evolves into hate, due to Macbeth's tyranny.

King Duncan is of good nature and both Macbeth, as well as Lady Macbeth, show conflict about killing him. However, King Duncan could also be faulted as he lacks the interpretive skills to understand his subjects and enemies. When King Duncan discovers that the Thane of Cawdor was a traitor he says of Cawdor "He was a gentleman on whom I built / An absolute trust." (1.4.14-15) At the beginning he questions a captain about the battle, relying on his answers and trusting two traitors, the Thane of Cawdor and Macdonald.

When King Duncan arrives at Macbeth's castle he is unable to see Lady Macbeth's true intention. This implies that King Duncan relies on his power and the loyalty of his subjects even though he can't keep a hold of his power. He relies on his divine right to rule and the protection of God even though he lacks the strength and perhaps the intelligence to stop the ambitious Macbeth and his wife.

4.4 Three Witches or Weïrd Sisters

The play begins with three witches who plan to meet Macbeth after a battle. When Macbeth arrives the witches tell him that he will be Thane of Cawdor and King of Scotland. When Macbeth revisits the witches and they show him three Apparitions:

---

[9] Lemon, Rebecca: Sovereignty and treason in Macbeth. in: Moschovakis, Nick (Hrsg.): Macbeth. New critical essays, Routledge, New York 2008, S. 74

An armed head, a bloody child and a child crowned with a tree in his hand. The Apparitions tell him to be aware of Macduff, that no man born of women can harm him and that he will only be defeated when Birnam Wood comes to Dunsinane.

In Shakespeare's time, many people were very interested in witches and the supernatural. One of these people was King James I, whose interest was awakened in 1591 when a group of witches and sorcerers attempted to murder him. Shakespeare knew that a play including witches would attract a large audience, including King James I himself.

"The weïrd sisters have been variously understood by different individuals, times, and cultures",[10] as the supernatural and the superstitious have been interpreted differently by different people, eras and cultures. The witches could represent how people can be tempted into evil or the witches could represent fate, Nick Moschovakis goes even as far to say that the witches embody "the unruly energies of desire, the pride of the great, and the manifold horrors of war and tyranny." Some of the witches' prophecies seem self-fulfilling, as it is very unlikely that Macbeth would have pursued the murder of King Duncan if the witches hadn't tempted him to, as Macbeth and his wife are too sure that the throne is destined for them, to ask what the witches' motives are. However, the prophecies of the apparitions seem to merely state the course of events.

At the end of the play, Macbeth is dead because of the cruel ambition that the witches planted in him and the audience is left to wonder whether or not the witches were merely prophesying the inevitable or toying with human lives, the cruel desire in all humans and embody unreasoning instinctive evil. The fact that the witches are beyond the limits of our comprehension has fascinated essayists and audiences to this day.

5 Conclusion

Macbeth was written around 1606 and is one of Shakespeare's most known plays. The plot centres on Macbeth and his wife who murder in order to rule Scotland. The play has entertained audiences for four centuries because the characters explore basic flaws that almost everyone can relate to. The character of Macbeth shows how a decent man can be tempted into evil and how difficult it is to tell the difference

---

[10] Moschovakis, Nick: Introduction. Dualistic *Macbeth*? Problematic *Macbeth*?. in: Moschovakis, Nick (Hrsg.): Macbeth. New critical essays, Routledge, New York 2008, S. 1 – 72

between good and evil. Both Macbeth and Lady Macbeth teach the lesson that an unhealthy ambition, guilt and self-doubt lead to unhappiness. Lady Macbeth could also be praise to powerful women. King Duncan relies on his power but is unable to stop the ambitious Macbeth and his wife. At the time, Shakespeare used the witches and the supernatural in order to gain the interest of the people of his time. On the other hand, the witches are so interesting because they are beyond the level of our comprehension as the audience is unsure whether or not they embody true evil or are just the agents of faith.

Shakespeare's *Macbeth* is made up of several complex characters that are all flawed in some way and maybe even teach the audience a lesson of some sort. They are one of the reasons why Shakespeare's works are still relevant and discussed to this day and why Shakespeare is seen as one of the greatest playwrights in the English language. As Ben Jonson wrote of Shakespeare "He was not of an age, but for all time."[11]

---

[11] http://www.shakespeareinamericancommunities.org/education/life-william-shakespeare, letzter Zugriff: 03.01.2016, 15:05

Sources

Bünsch, Iris u.a.: William Shakespeare Macbeth. Reclam, Stuttgart 2004

Lemon, Rebecca: Sovereignty and treason in Macbeth. in: Moschovakis, Nick (Hrsg.): Macbeth. New critical essays, Routledge, New York 2008, S. 73 – 87

Moschovakis, Nick: Introduction. Dualistic *Macbeth*? Problematic *Macbeth*?, in: Moschovakis, Nick (Hrsg.): Macbeth. New critical essays, Routledge, New York 2008, S. 1 – 72

Mühlmann, Horst: William Shakespeare Macbeth. Klett Lernen und Wissen, 4. verbesserte Aufl., Stuttgart 2010

Sabin, Stefana: Shakespeare auf 100 Seiten. Reclam, Stuttgart 2014

Shakespeare, William: Macbeth. Gibson, Rex (Hrsg.) Cambridge University Press, Cambridge 2005

http://www.shakespeareinamericancommunities.org/education/life-william-shakespeare, letzter Zugriff: 03.01.2016, 15:05

http://www.biography.com/people/william-shakespeare-9480323, letzter Zugriff: 06.01, 17:30

http://www.william-shakespeare.info/elizabethan-women.htm, letzter Zugriff: 10.01.2016, 11:15

http://www.cummingsstudyguides.net/xMacbeth.html, letzter Zugriff: 03.01.2016, 16:30

http://www.sparknotes.com/shakespeare/macbeth/canalysis.html, letzter Zugriff: 04.01.2016, 18:10

YOUR KNOWLEDGE HAS VALUE

- We will publish your bachelor's and master's thesis, essays and papers

- Your own eBook and book - sold worldwide in all relevant shops

- Earn money with each sale

Upload your text at www.GRIN.com
and publish for free